九字印

Ku　　*Ji*　　*In*

Kuji-In Teacher's Guide

By Acharya MahaVajra

Venerable Great Lightning

Copyright François Lépine © 2008

ISBN 978-0-9809415-4-8

Table of Content

Teacher Preparation

Before you can become a certified teacher of Kuji-In in the Transformational Approach, a few things must have been covered.

1- You must have read all the 3 books of the Kuji-In trilogy from François Lépine, and have practiced each technique at least a few times, including all Qi-Gong techniques found in the first book. You may use your own experience and Qi-Gong teachings in your own class, but must be aware of the standard teachings.

2- You must have done the 9 Day Kuji-In Meditation process, and the 63 Hour Kuji-In Self-Initiation process, found at the end of the second book.

3- Altar, prayer and mala charge, at least once a week, preferably every day. You must have started this process when you request your teacher certification, and you will have to do it before each time you teach Kuji-In, in addition to your daily or weekly practice.

Without requiring that you become a Buddhist in a religious way, you must build yourself a simple spiritual altar in the tradition of your choice (Buddhist, Christian, Hindu…). Sitting in front of your altar, make a prayer of gratitude towards the God of your belief. Then, use a mala to recite 108 times a single Kuji-In mantra of your choice, using the Sanskrit version of the mantras.

A mala is a Buddhist or Hindu prayer necklace, made of 108 beads. You count each bead for each time you recite a mantra. While holding a mala, you will not be making the mudra with your hands. Chanting a mantra 108 times, using the mala to count, will empower the mala with the consciousness of the mantra, and will support your energy and your spiritual elevation when you teach. You should not use your index finger to count the mala beads, but use your major finger or your thumb. The more you chant Kuji-In mantras using your mala, the stronger the effect will be.

No one but yourself should touch your personal mala. Although it is not dramatic, you will have to re-do a mala to reinstate the full power of your mala.

More information about the use of a mala is available at the end of this booklet, in the "Master Preparation" chapter.

Initiation

When any spiritual teaching is passed from master to disciple or from teacher to student, there is also a passing of consciousness, where the student's spirit is receptive to the spirit of the teacher, and an "initiation" occurs. What happens is that part of the knowledge and experience of the teacher is passed to the student, so that the student does not have to spend hundreds of hours before he can gain consciousness of the spiritual teaching. This initiation permits the student to become aware almost immediately of the sacred teaching, almost up to the level of consciousness that the teacher has of such teaching. Then, the student must still build up his own experience of the teaching, by practice, so that he can fully illume himself from this spiritual consciousness.

YET, before any spiritual teaching existed, before the concept of empowerment was used, there were humans on a spiritual quest that spent many hundreds of hours in meditation and spiritual practice, hoping to discover themselves, and discover the spiritual world. Thus, it is possible for anyone to discover any spiritual teaching by studying and practicing by themselves even if it takes

MUCH more time, a self-empowerment will occur, with time, practice and perseverance.

The goal of other-empowerment, or to receive initiation from a master, is to produce such an extreme shift in consciousness that the perception of the student is awakened in order to feel and live the experience immediately. Without this immediate experience of the spiritual truth, the student might start to think it is useless... and eventually drop his spiritual practice.

Once someone has gone through a few processes of empowerment with a master, over a long enough period of time, the consciousness of the student, now awakened, can get immediate self-empowerment because of the availability of the human self to participate in the spiritual practice with the spirit-true-self. New monks and students are taught by masters, but advanced students and masters study alone. They read the scriptures alone, pray alone, and join the spirit world alone, where they self-empower themselves. For example, when the highest master of a lineage studies and practices, he still gains power, he does not need anyone else to teach him, because he lets himself to be touched by the Buddhas and the Bodhisattvas directly; or he joins himself as human and spirit, as one, where all is the same, and all the consciousness of all things is the consciousness of all other things. Christian practitioners of Kuji-In get in contact with the Father, the Christ, and the Holy Spirit.

To review: initiation is the process where a master or teacher empowers someone else, to assist the seeker on his path, to show the spiritual way, and to accelerate the process of awakening. Such a process is greatly encouraged, but is not necessary to illume oneself or to find the inner-truth. Throughout history, a great deal of saints and masters awakened themselves simply because they spent a lot of time focusing on the God of their religion, or on the sprit-self, with devotion and faith.

In Kuji-In, we learn that there are no space and time, no dimension outside of illusion. Thus, having distant initiation, via email or phone, is almost as efficient as an initiation with direct contact. Reading the books will lead you so far, but you will need either a lot of practice, or previous spiritual experience. If you already "transcended" while in meditation, every spiritual concept passed, even thru the reading of spiritual books, will touch you and will inspire you.

Learning from books takes more time, yet it is a reasonable alternative when a master is not accessible. I teach this even in the books that I wrote myself. Some of my on-line students advance faster in their spiritual development than some of my 4-wall class students, because it does not depend as much on the proximity of the contact, than on the availability of the students to be touched by spirit. The "transcendental" experience of Retsu will help a teacher understand this non-dimension aspect of the universe.

So that an initiative process can occur, it is very important to meditate regularly, and to practice the techniques that will be passed on, if only for a moment, before teaching them, so to awaken the energy within the body and the experience of it in the teacher's consciousness.

Earnings

It is reasonable to earn payments in exchange for the teachings given. For ages, when students and disciples went to the temple to learn, they brought some food, and spent some time working around the temple, in exchange for the wisdom they would receive. Today, this exchange is balanced by money, most of the time, but the exchange is not required to be monetary. However, there must be some form of respectful exchange.

The exchange must be balanced, and must not be burdening for the student or the teacher. If there is ego, arrogance or abuse in the exchange, it should not take place. Be wise and follow your heart, as well as your discernment. Teachers are allowed to earn a living.

Teachers and Masters may purchase material (books, prayer malas…) from F.Lepine Publishing at discount prices, to sell to their students at regular price.

Environment

The environment must be suitable to exchange spiritual wisdom. The place should be clean enough, comfortable, with reasonable air quality. There should be enough room for each student to practice standing Qi-Gong, such as the Dance of the Dragon, or other Qi-Gong practice that the teacher knows. The room temperature must be comfortable, not too cold, not too hot. However, in any case, do your best with the available means.

Dress code

Students should be dressed comfortably, so that their breathing is fluid and unhindered while standing and sitting. Some martial art and Qi-Gong schools may provide a kimono or standard vestment. Clothing should be not too cold, not to hot. A teacher or master should wear something significant to their title during class. It can be simple clothing that reflects Zen neutrality, or Tai-Chi style.

Altar

There should be an altar in the teaching class, or at least, a spiritual statue displayed in a respectful way. Depending on your spiritual path, it can be a Buddha, a Christ or a Shiva. People should not be allowed to run past the altar without respect, when learning Kuji-In.

The altar should be composed according to the teacher's beliefs and ways, but always in a respectful manner. Do not place weapons on the altar unless they are held by a Buddha or an angel. If you place offerings of food and water, do not let them sit too long, until they lose their freshness. Better to have no offerings than rotting ones.

Air and Bones

Each Kuji-In practice or class must include breathing exercises, of any type, for at least a few breaths. While in class, students tend to dislike doing long periods of breathing, so you can insist on having a few conscious breaths, and encourage them to practice for a few minutes at home.

Each Kuji-In practice or class must include, from time to time, Qi-Gong exercises to help the energy flow thru the body, and some exercises to add flexibility to the spine. The Dance of the Dragon is totally appropriate for such a purpose. Start by teaching the movements of the hands in the "3-loop 8-shape", then add the swaying of the hips, then the orientation of the head and hands. Students should be allowed to advance to their own rhythm and abilities, as they grasp each new step of the technique.

Preparation

Before each class or seminar, the teacher should take a small amount of time to engage the energies of Kuji-In in his/her body. Before a class of 1 hour, a few minutes will suffice. Before a 2 day seminar, at least 1 hour of prayer and practice must be done. Or else, the teacher might unknowingly deplete his energy. Advanced students should sweep the floor or tend to the new students if need be. This preparation should not be taken on the class time, and should not be done in ways to attract the attention of new students. Humility is recommended. (I personally breathe and pray alone, before each class, while advanced students sweep the floor for a few minutes.).

Progression

Teachers must start by teaching adequate breathing techniques, and quickly go to the feeling of the Qi. Respect the pace of your students. It is not essential for them to actually feel the Qi to continue, but they should at least learn the basic techniques.

A Kuji-In set should be taught first using the basic tools, such as the Japanese syllable (RIN, KYO, TOH…), and add the Sanskrit prayer only when the student learned all other aspects of the Set. Each class should cover the philosophy of a Kuji-In technique, as well as the ritual aspect. When students have learned the first level of philosophy and ritual practice, for each of the nine Kuji-In sets, then they should be taught the advanced techniques, then the Mastery techniques.

The techniques from the first book are introductive. In the second book, you go more profound. The mudra is the same. It is the technique that evolves at a higher level. In the third book, you'll see another level of techniques, slightly different from the 1st and second book. If you wish to become a competent teacher, you have to learn them all, so you can lead others thru the process progressively. The first time we practice the Kuji-In, it has to be easy and soft. Then, in the advanced training, we go stronger, with more details, and we insist on learning the Sanskrit mantras by heart. At the mastery level, you'll see a deeper sense of the Kuji-In, that you should not transmit to beginners.

Weekly class

While you should find a method that fits your style, I will give an example of how I teach in the format of a weekly class. Once you understand the main structure, you can adapt it to your preferences.

When I give weekly class, I accept new students at any time, and give a continuous course, adapting to the level of each new student, and advanced student present. Thus, a new student could start learning in the Retsu class, and it would be fine, since the first time a student attends a class, he learns an aspect of the philosophy and the basic ritual application in a half-meditative state. Once a student has seen all of the nine Kuji-In sets, both in philosophy and ritual application, he can continue learning all the various philosophical aspects and higher levels of application of the techniques. I always give the choice to advanced students (9 weeks or more) to attend the philosophical exposé again, at another level, or to go in the back to practice the Kuji-In set's ritual using the Sanskrit prayer for 20 minutes, to feel the empowerment. When a student attends a Kuji-In set class for a second time, or after multiple encounters, I give him a sheet of the reviewed Kuji-In set, printed from Book 1. In an intensive seminar, I give all participants a set of 9 sheets printed from book 1. While I encourage each Kuji-In student to purchase their own set of books, all should have access to the reminder when they learn the technique with a teacher or master. Teachers and masters have permission to print copies of the 9 Kuji-In pages from book 1 (the 9 pages with the photos of the mudras and the mantras), to distribute to their students.

I start a class with a simple breathing period, of about 1 minute, where I teach normal and reversed breathing to new students, while other students simply practice. This goes on for only a minute or two, and then I continue with Qi-Gong training for a few more minutes (10-15 minutes). Then, I start giving philosophy that will concern the Kuji-In set of the day. The first day of class will cover RIN, with a philosophy either of self-trust, courage, faith, right to live... Then, the following week with KYO, I will speak either of responsibility, of affirming what you want to create, of the karmic implications of our actions, of the power of benediction and malediction,... on the third week, TOH, I might speak of giving myself attention, of understanding myself, of auto-therapy, of introspection...

Once the philosophy was explained (15-20 minutes), I start teaching the ritual aspect of the weekly Kuji-In set. For RIN, I show the correct application of the mudra, and give only the Japanese syllable mantra. I invite the students to practice this way for 2 minutes. Then, I will ask them to add the focus on the base chakra. While they continue their practice, I will speak softly "Rin.... Rin... Rin... Base chakra". Then I will invite them to imagine that their base chakra is setting aflame, and that the flame rises in their body and around it. I reapeat something like "Rin... Rin... Rin... Base chakra, feel it... it is aflme, your entire body is aflame and purified... Rin... Rin... Rin..." and keep silent for 1 more minute. Then I will ask them to add to their focus, a feeling of self-trust, or right to live. And I will repeat softly the tools to focus on. It is easy to keep the mudra, so we must simply utter the other elements of the practice: "Rin... Rin... Rin... base chakra is the focus and source of the fire... your entire body aflame,... Self-trust... birthright to live...".

After 10 minutes focusing on the RIN basic application of the ritual, I ask them to open their eyes and be at peace. I quickly review without insisting the 5 tools that compose the RIN Kuji-In set:

- Show the mudra again
- RIN to be repeated mentally
- Base chakra to focus
- Visualize to body on fire, set by the base chakra
- Nourish a feeling of self-trust

Then, I ask them if any of them have any question. They usually don't have any, their mind numbed by the Kuji-In practice that generated serotonin and endorphin in their brain. So I will pick a random subject, about breathing or Qi-Gong, so that they come back to a natural state of mind. This helps them integrate the teaching more easily.

This procedure allows for a continuous teaching, to always add new students to the class, and cover many philosophical aspects of each Kuji-In set over a year of teaching, never seeming to give the same class. The Qi-Gong techniques being slightly different from class to class, with only the Dance of the Dragon persisting, and the 8-9 week laps before a Kuji-In set is taught again. I wrote 8-9 weeks because sometimes, when students prefer tangible subject, I will give ZAI and ZEN one after the other, during the same class. When students prefer the spiritual approach, ZAI and ZEN are covered separately, while ZEN includes little explanation and longer meditation periods.

Some of your students will not practice at home, using a weekly class to take a break from the material based world. Other students will practice at home, knowing that practice is the key to success. It is not essential for your students to go thru the 63 hour self-initiation before they acquire "Mastery" level information. It will simply make less sense for them, and be less efficient. The self-initiation must be explained, but not imposed. (It is necessary for you, as a teacher, to have done it, if you want to teach high-level Kuji-In, so that your energy will assist your student's awakening). Experienced students should learn and practice the Sanskrit mantras of each Kuji-In level.

In any case, follow your intuition and follow the needs of the group. Do not be so arrogant as to follow a preset plan and ignore the feeling of the group. You should prepare yourself before each class then follow the intuition generated by the student's spiritual needs. However, if a student seeks attention too much, or victimizes to hinder the progress of the entire group, deal with it responsibly and offer to the majority what they need. You are not a savior or a therapist.

Seminars

Seminars are handled in the same order as a class, but over a different period of time. If you read the above, then you will understand the following bullet points:

-   Welcome the students to the seminar. Presentations.
-   Breathing, various ways
-   Qi-Gong, feeling chi, Dance of the Dragon (or Qi-Gong of your choice)
-   Pause
-   Brief history of Kuji-In
-   Explain: mudra, mantra, mandala (visualization), chakra, dharma (philosophy)
-   Philosophy for RIN
-   Ritual basics for RIN
-   Philosophy for KYO
-   Ritual basics for KYO
-   Break
-   Philosophy and ritual basics for TOH, then SHA
-   Break
-   KAI, JIN
-   Break
-   RETSU, ZAI and ZEN
-   Break

- Meditation
- Overview of the seminar
- Last question period

Pauses can be short or long. They can be 10-20 minutes breaks, or meal times, or entire nights for seminars going over more than 1 day. In any case, adapt the pauses to fit the feeling of the group, and to follow their evolution thru the process, and give them time to assimilate the information as well as the energy.

Here and there, question periods should be allowed. Be diligent with students who wish to attract attention and disturb the on-going of the seminar ("We will speak of this at a later time,… now let's go on with the KAI philosophy").

You can arrange seminars to separate Basic, Advanced and Mastery level teachings, to follow the books, or (my preference) have ongoing seminars every few weeks/months, where people always learn new stuff. In the latter situation, prepare some material for Advanced and Mastery students, so that they can practice while you give the class to new students.

When returning from a pause of any length, let your students do a few conscious breaths. When returning from a night's sleep, do breathing and Qi-Gong again, to restart the energies.

It is encouraged to offer the first book of the Kuji-In trilogy, as a reminder, at the end of the seminar. It may be included in the seminar fees. However, the learning process should be done without any help from books, or notepads, to encourage the brain to put energy in the learning process. Explain to your students that learning from a certified teacher is more than 10 times efficient as learning on our own, from books.

Titles

In any case, you may use titles that you have earned if you wish, without giving too much importance to your titles. You are equal to each of your students. Do not allow yourself to compare or compete. Arrogance is not a trait of a Kuji-In teacher, even less a Kuji-In Master.

Use your titles only to reassure students who request proof of your competence. Do not insist however, when these titles are not even asked. Titles should be briefly mentioned in first presentations, if it seems necessary, or in a seminar introduction.

Tradition

While I do not insist on the traditional Buddhist religious dogma behind Kuji-In, I do insist that the training process respects the traditional ways. To follow these ways, the teachings should be given approximately the way Kuji-In is taught throughout the Kuji-In trilogy of books. I encourage each teacher to put their own experiences into their teaching, but to be careful about it. Some teachers added so much of their experience that there was no more Kuji-In, but puzzles of mudras and magic formulas, that did not lead the students thru a proper evolution of the Kuji-In process in their body and mind.

Until you become a Spiritual Master, you should not go too far away from the Kuji-In that was taught to you thru the Transformational Approach, consolidated by François Lépine in various forms and media, but created by the elders and pioneers of Hindu Esoteric Buddhism. Yourself being a martial art master, or a good holistic healer, does not make you a Spiritual Master.

Teaching Material

As a Kuji-In Teacher or Master of the Transformational Approach, you have the right to purchase Kuji-In books and videos at 50% of the regular price, and to sell these to your students at the regular price, for them to use as guidelines.

You do not have the right to copy, duplicate or produce any material that is the property of F.Lepine Publishing, without permission.

However, all certified teachers and masters have permission to photocopy pages from the first book of the trilogy that cover the basics of Kuji-In (9 pages only, from RIN to ZEN), for students that already went thru these teachings for the second time, or in seminar, and only for students that have paid (or given exchange) to receive these reminders. These copies are to serve only as reminders to another form of teaching, and it should be encouraged that each student owns their own copy of the first book of the trilogy, if not the entire trilogy.

Certifications

As a teacher, you have the right to offer certificates to your students, to indicate they have successfully attended a seminar on Kuji-In, or followed thru a set of classes. The certificate can be the one offered from François Lépine along with the teacher certification or one of your own creation. In this case, your certificate should indicate the "Transformational Approach from Kuji-In Master François Lépine" and a seal of your school.

Only a certified Kuji-In Master may offer Teacher and Master certification. Until a Master can sense the level of energy and the evolution of a student with great precision, he should not give teacher certifications to a student before the student has 3 years of practice. A Master who does not feel the evolution of a being simply cannot certify another teacher to become a Master.

Disclaimer

François Lépine was ordained in the Pureland tradition of Hangaku Jodo, a Pure Land Buddhist lineage from Japan. Being a North-American, he speaks French and English, and does not speak Japanese. The Buddha did not speak Japanese either, but Sanskrit and local languages, and according to his instructions, we are to adapt the Buddhist teachings to each new circumstance and culture.

François Lépine tracked down the origins of the Japanese Kuji-In to the Chinese Nine Seals, and then back to India, the homeland of the Buddha, leading to the wisdom of Vajrayana, a Buddhist way of invoking the power within. It was originally a Hindu ritual of sacrifice towards the Hindu God Indra, but the reference to the gods being removed from the Buddhist wisdom, we invoke the Force and sublime Energy of the higher-self.

No belonging to any specific organization is required to learn and benefit from this wisdom. It is not required to become a Japanese, Chinese or Tibetan to practice any form of Buddhism. François Lépine's publications were called Kuji-In because it is thru this appellation that it was made popular around the world.

In all your perceptions, you are encouraged to see the higher wisdom that usually does not conform to any tradition, trend, cultural environment, tradition or system of belief. The soul and the spirit world are not bound by natural laws, nor by human definitions.

Teacher Certification

When you feel ready to request your official certification as a Kuji-In teacher in the Transformational Approach, you may do so on the website www.Kujiin.com.

Master preparation

Receiving the title of "Kuji-In Master" means that you master the ritual technique of Kuji-In, but also the philosophical path of Kuji-In. This title does not make you a Spiritual Master, but acknowledges your competence in Kuji-In. Authentic Vajrayana Buddhist teachings can only be taught by an ordained Buddhist priest. In this sense, you must know the distinction between teaching the Kuji-In technique, and teaching the Buddhist path. If you cannot find a Vajrayana Buddhist close to you, you may contact François Lépine for more information on his on-line Buddhist teachings. However, Buddhism is not required to practice a spiritual technique, and a few students of the Transformational Approach already adapted Kuji-In to their Christian path.

Emotional Transmutation:

The most powerful technique of Kuji-In is hidden in the Emotional Transmutation, and recognition of the ego. A Kuji-In teacher that aspires to become a Kuji-In Master, must practice Emotional Transmutation (found in book 2) at least one hundred times. It can be practiced every day or once a week, or when the teacher feels like it. This experience will elevate the energy and spirit of the teacher if at the end of each practice, attention is put on joy and peace. This technique might sink someone into depression if the attention is left on the dark feelings and emotions. Practice the technique like it was taught in the book. Go to the depths of each situation, then, come back up.

Emotional transmutation is meant to clear the passage, but then, you have to keep the passage clean. You must also take time to recognize what actions you took, what words you said, and what thoughts you kept in mind, so that the emotional situation happened. It is by recognizing the methods used by the ego to sabotage your heart that you will become a master.

If you are afraid of a monster in the closet, go sit in the closet, close the door, sit in the dark with your monster, and feel the monster thru and thru. Then, come back to joy. Then, look at your ego, and at the illusion it pushes on your mind, to flee from the truth that you see in yourself. Be at peace.

Even when you have experience with Emotional Transmutation, you are not allowed to play the therapist with anyone you encounter. Even if you see their situation, it does not mean you must tell them. Follow discernment and be responsible for your own evolution.

Charging the mantras:

A Kuji-In master must be charged with the consciousness contained in the Sanskrit mantras of Kuji-In. You must acquire a prayer mala (Buddhist mala, made of wood, 108 beads, or Hindu mala, made of rudraksha beads, 109 beads).

The expression "to do a mala" means that you repeat a mantra 108 times, using your mala to count. Using a mala, to count mantras, we call this technique "japa". On the Hindu mala, we do not count the 109th bead, reserved to Vishnu or Shiva. You must not jump over the 109th bead, but reverse the direction of your Hindu mala and do your next mala in the other direction. Buddhist malas with 108 beads are not concerned by this rule.

When you count your mantras using a mala (doing japa), you are progressively charging the mala to make it into a power item, a talisman that will keep your energy high anytime you wear it. You should count your beads using your major or your thumb. You must not touch your mala with your index while doing japa. It is not dramatic, but it would un-charge the energy previously charged in the mala. Counting using your index would charge your body with the mantra, but not the mala itself. Touching your mala with your index while not reciting mantras has very little discharging effect, so don't worry when you manipulate your mala to put it on or take it off. Store your mala in a sacred place, on an altar or in a blessed pouch. When you wear it, keep it inside your clothing.

Then, the expression "to do 9 malas" means that you use your mala to repeat 9 times 108 mantras. Before you can become a Kuji-In Master, you must have charged yourself of 108 malas of each of the 9 Kuji-In Sanskrit mantras. For 12 days in a row, chant 9 malas of the RIN level Sanskrit mantra, while softly contemplating the meaning (trust / faith), without effort. You must not miss out on a single day, or else, you have to start to charge this mantra all over again. Once you have chanted 9 malas per day for 12 days, totaling 108 malas, you will have chanted 11664 times the first mantra of Kuji-In. Give yourself a few days of break, if you wish to, and do the same process with the KYO Sanskrit mantra, while contemplating its meaning (responsibility / universal circulation).

Before each of your japa sessions, you must do a prayer to elevate yourself spiritually. For each of the 9 Sanskrit mantras of Kuji-In, you will have chanted 11664 times the mantra, in the form of 9 malas per day for 12 days in a row, resulting in a built up charge in your body and consciousness. Once you have charged a mantra this way, the concept will not leave you, ever, unless you make effort to make it leave (but why would you?!). When reciting the Kuji-In mantras in japa technique, you don't do the mudra with your hands, and the visualization is accessory. The state of mind and the mantra are most important while doing japa. When you notice you are thinking of other things, simply continue doing your japa and come back to contemplating the philosophy. It is normal that your mind will want to waver; you have to train at mastering yourself, without judging yourself.

At times during your practice, you might transcend. You will think you fell asleep, but you did not. Transcending is when your consciousness leaves your body to go to a higher state of existence, and comes back after. It is recommended to transcend while meditating, but it is not very useful while you are trying to charge a mantra. If you tend to transcend during your japa recitation, do your malas standing up, walking around gently, to prevent yourself from losing consciousness. If you drop your mala and lose count, go back around 10 beads back, and restart from there. You can use a paper pad to note each mala completed. If you lose count of your malas, make one more, just in case.

The mantra can be recited in your mind or whispering. The speed of recitation of the mantra is the speed at which you can say it with your voice, while each syllable is said correctly. Some people like to "speed-dial" their mantras, because it goes faster and it still has the charging effect. The mantra must be audible and correctly spelled if you say it aloud. With practice, you will be able to chant your mantras fast enough. You will be able to do 9 malas in less then 30 minutes.

With all the mantras charged, it is you that is charged, your own consciousness, and your energy system that is circulating with these energies. It you ever lose or break your mala, it does not mean you have to start over the entire charge. It only means that you have broken the power item that you created when you charged the mantras. You cannot lose what is inside you. But, it is a good thing to keep a charged mala.

If you have other questions about the japa technique, most of the time, the answer is to practice in a sacred state of mind, and practice again.

The 9 x 12 formula is applicable to mantras of a single line. Mantras of a few lines are to be practiced 1 mala per day, for 41 days. We do not have paragraph long mantras in Kuji-In, but we do have some in Vajrayana, which is the Buddhism that contains Kuji-In. Contact a Kuji-In Master or a Buddhist priest to receive more information about this Buddhist path.

About MahaVajra

MahaVajra (born François Lépine) is a Buddhist Bishop in the Mahajrya tradition, entitled to open official Buddhist temples and ordain priests. He is the founder of Quantum Buddhism, a modern Buddhist way compatible with new scientific discoveries in the field of Quantum Physics. He was ordained as Bishop (*Acharya*, in Sanskrit) in the official lineage of Pure Land Buddhism. He added his experience of Vajrayana to the Quantum Buddhism teachings, and founded the Mahajrya esoteric tradition.

Acharya MahaVajra means Most-Reverend Great Diamond / Thunderbolt / Lightning / Adamentium. The meaning of the Sanskrit word Vajra is numberless, and refers to power and indestructibility.

He is also one of the founders of the Mystic Knighthood, a community of spiritual warriors that promote virtuous behavior, free-will, and self mastery. This community is preferred by martial artists, but counts many healers and scholars.

Quantum Buddhism: http://www.QuantumBuddhism.org

Mystic Knighthood: http://www.MysticKnight.org

On-line teaching website: http://www.MasterWithin.org

Main website: http://www.flepine.com

www.ingramcontent.com/pod-product-compliance
Lightning Source LLC
Chambersburg PA
CBHW071637050426
42443CB00028B/3401